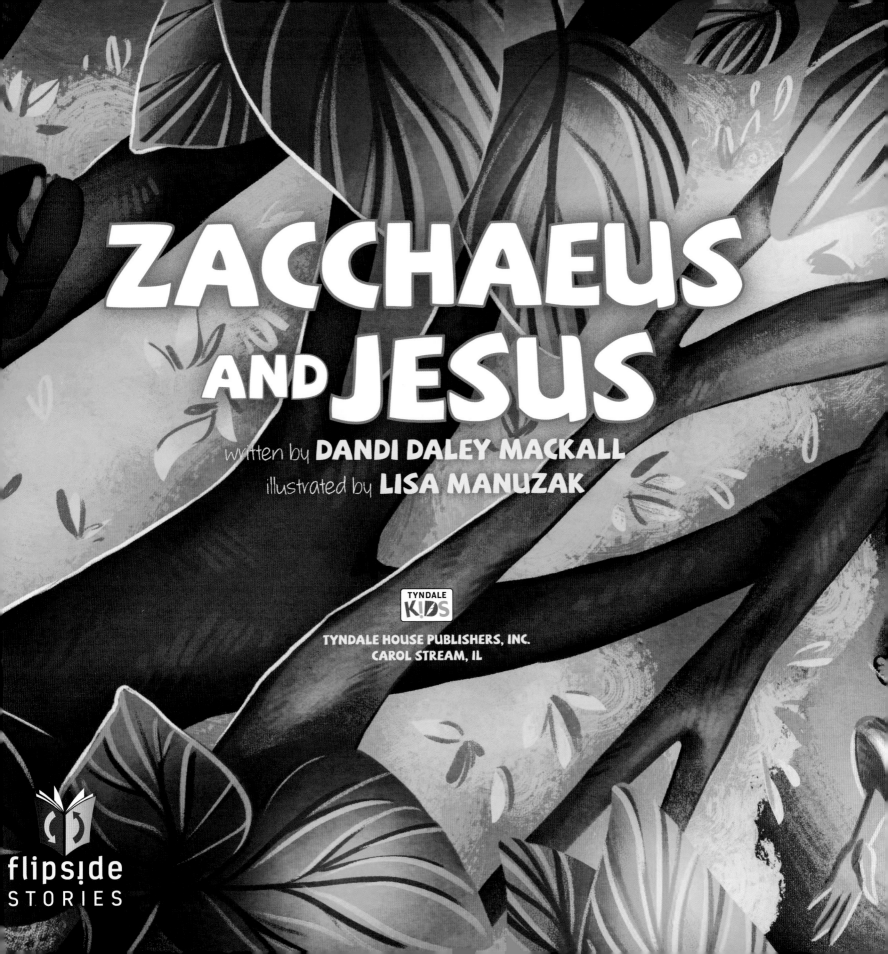

ZACCHAEUS
AND JESUS

written by **DANDI DALEY MACKALL**

illustrated by **LISA MANUZAK**

TYNDALE
KIDS

TYNDALE HOUSE PUBLISHERS, INC.
CAROL STREAM, IL

flipside
STORIES

To Maddie Mackall—
welcome!

Visit Tyndale's website for kids at www.tyndale.com/kids.

TYNDALE is a registered trademark of Tyndale House Publishers, Inc. The Tyndale Kids logo is a trademark of Tyndale House Publishers, Inc.

Zacchaeus and Jesus

Copyright © 2016 by Dandi A. Mackall. All rights reserved.

Illustrations copyright © Lisa Manuzak. All rights reserved.

Designed by Jacqueline L. Nuñez

Edited by Stephanie Rische

Scripture quotations are taken from the *Holy Bible*, New Living Translation, copyright © 1996, 2004, 2015 by Tyndale House Foundation. Used by permission of Tyndale House Publishers, Inc., Carol Stream, Illinois 60188. All rights reserved.

For manufacturing information regarding this product, please call 1-800-323-9400.

ISBN 978-1-4964-1119-8

Printed in China

22	21	20	19	18	17	16
7	6	5	4	3	2	1

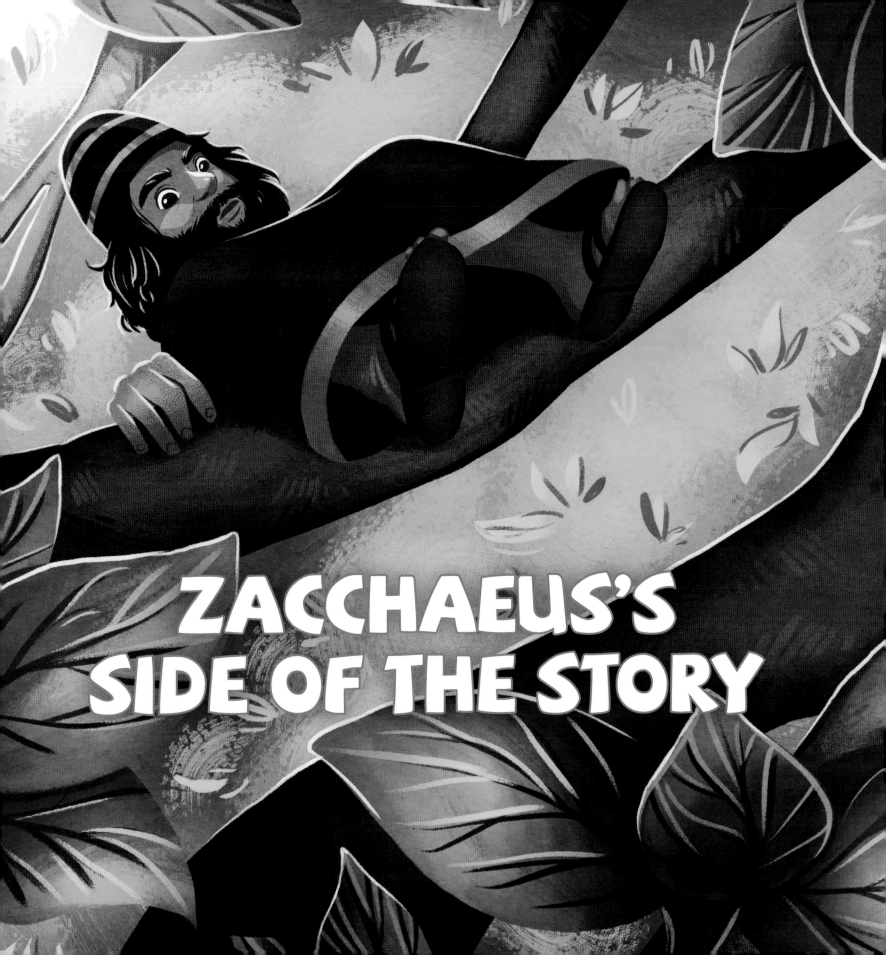

ZACCHAEUS'S SIDE OF THE STORY

I'm "Shorty" Zacchaeus. The crowds know my name.
My job: collect taxes. I make it a game.
The Romans get rich. And Zacchaeus?
The same!

2

But lately, I've heard about Jesus.

5

They say He's God's Son—could it really be true?
They claim that He healed a blind beggar or two,
Made thousands of loaves out of only a few.

I like what I've heard about Jesus.

8

"He's coming! It's Jesus!" The shouts reach my ears.
"He's passing through Jericho! Give Him three cheers!"
I race to the pathway in case He appears.

I think that I'd like to see Jesus.

The city has gathered, and crowds line the street.
My money can't buy me a good ringside seat.
I wish I were taller—I only see feet.

I must find a way to see Jesus.

12

I jump and I shove, but I still cannot see!
I look through the branches that reach down to me.
That's it! So I climb up the sycamore tree.

I hope that from here I'll see Jesus.

I see Him! That's Jesus—He's coming my way!
He stops and looks up. Then I hear my Lord say,
"Zacchaeus, come down! I'm your guest for today."

I climb down so I can meet Jesus.

16

A man in the crowd shouts, "You can't be his guest!
He's taken our taxes and stolen the rest.
So why should that sinner Zacchaeus be blessed?"

They're right. And I can't look at Jesus.

"I ask Your forgiveness. I'll settle the score.
I'll take half my money and give to the poor.
For each one I've cheated, I'll pay four
times more."

Now all that I want is my Jesus.

21

I'll never forget what I learned on this day.
I'm thankful for Jesus, who shows me the way.
I feel ten feet tall! Now I want to obey!

We walk home, just me and my Jesus.

JESUS' SIDE OF THE STORY

I'm Jesus of Nazareth, God's only Son.
I lived on the earth till My mission was done.
I came for all people—Zacchaeus was one.

God sent Me to those who were lost.

While traveling west, My disciples and I,
We stopped in at Jericho, not passing by.
I knew they all wondered, but no one
   asked why.

I was looking for those who were lost.

5

6

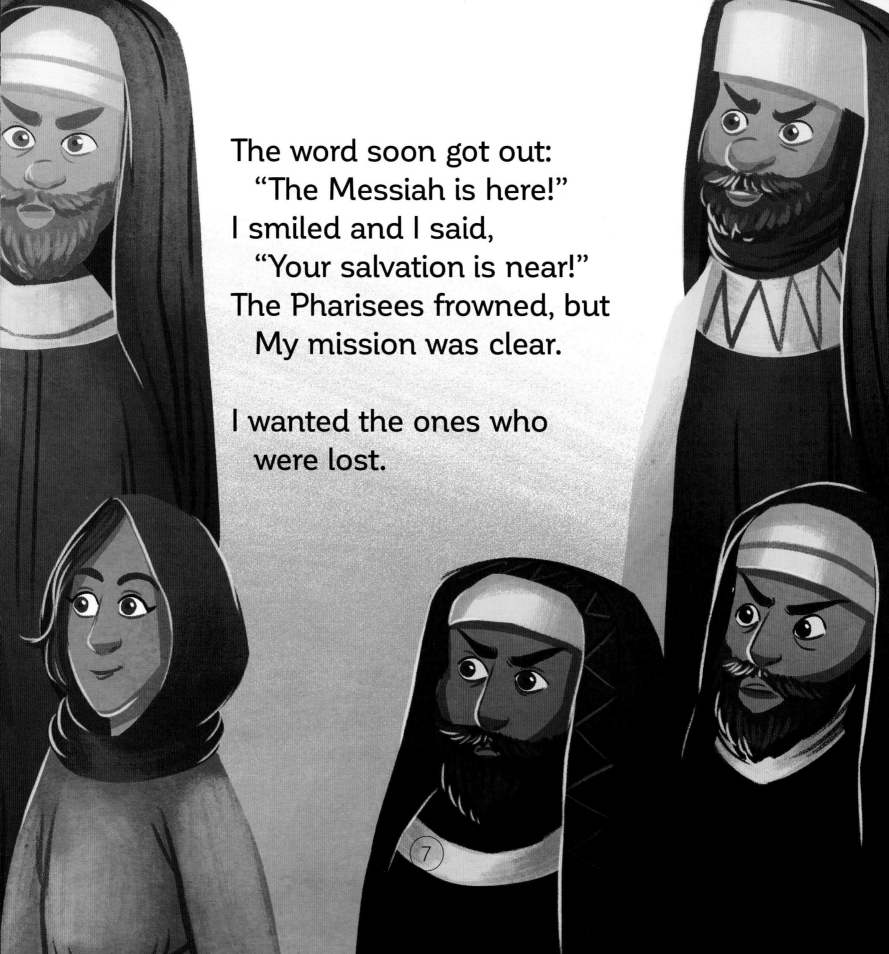

The word soon got out:
  "The Messiah is here!"
I smiled and I said,
  "Your salvation is near!"
The Pharisees frowned, but
  My mission was clear.

I wanted the ones who
  were lost.

7

I spotted one man who was climbing a tree.
His legs were so short that he couldn't see Me.
I knew the man's heart, how he longed to be free—

Zacchaeus, the one who was lost.

We moved with the crowd. Then I stopped in the
   street.
"So why is He stopping? It must be the heat."
 I answered, "There's someone I've come here to
   meet—

Zacchaeus, the one who is lost."

I watched My disciples, confused
as could be.
They looked all around and then
stared back at Me.
I grinned and gazed up in the
sycamore tree,

Seeking the man who was lost.

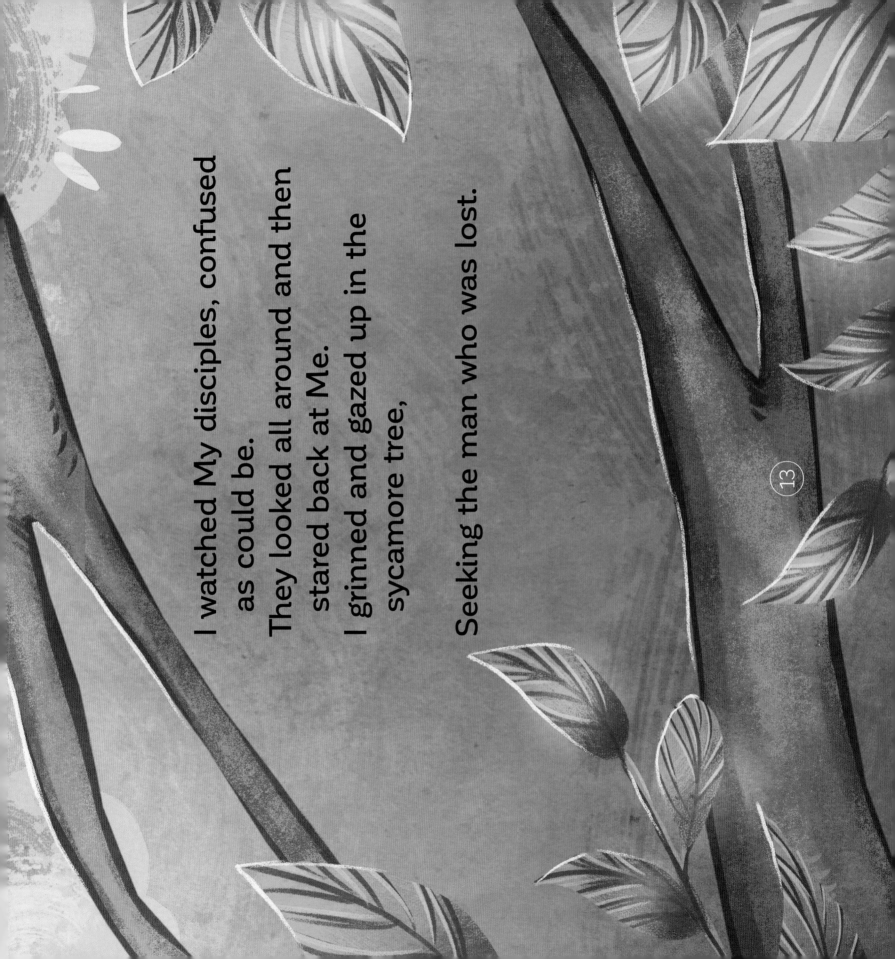

13

"Zacchaeus, come down! I'm your guest for today!"
He scurried right down. We backed out of his way.
"You'd come to my house? Might I beg You to stay?"

Stay with the one who was lost?

"Not fair!" the crowd yelled. "He's the
    worst in the land!
He's richer than rich, and his palace is
    grand!
He cheats us!" they shouted.
    "You don't understand."

Zacchaeus was lonely and lost.

I told them Zacchaeus deserved a fresh start.
"I know that this man's had a true change of heart!
Let's love one another, and all do our part

To seek and to save all the lost!"

The man kept his promise to pay back the poor.
He asked their forgiveness and settled the score.
The Kingdom of God grew one citizen more.

Salvation had come to the lost!

*The Son of Man came to seek
and save those who are lost.*

LUKE 19:10